Grow the Best Asparagus

Michael Higgins

CONTENTS

GW00391700

Introduction

In the early spring, when other fresh vegetables are unavailable, how pleasant it is to have one of the tastiest vegetables ready to harvest. And it is reassuring to know that the harvest will continue each spring for years to come. A well-prepared asparagus bed, in good soil, should produce abundantly for up to twenty-five years. If you can be patient in the beginning, you will be rewarded by a wonderful return for your labor.

A gourmet treat, expensive when purchased (and never as fresh), asparagus can be grown in almost any garden where there is a cold or dry season to provide it with a dormant period. As a vegetable, the versatile asparagus can be cooked in many ways and dried, canned, or frozen for off-season eating. Low in calories, high in flavor, each serving of four spears (sixty grams) contains only ten calories, with two grams of carbohydrates and one gram of protein. Asparagus is a very good source of thiamin and a good source of vitamin A and riboflavin.

The asparagus plant is a beautiful addition to any location. Few garden sights are more attractive than early dew glistening in the feathery, dark green foliage of the summer plants. In the fall, the asparagus fern turns a bright yellow, and when snow is on the ground, the light brown brush bends high over the white.

Where Did It Come From?

Asparagus grows wild in so many areas throughout the world that it is hard to pinpoint its place of origin. Both the Greeks and the Romans cultivated the plant. In fact, when the Romans wanted to indicate a very short time, they would say, "In the time it takes to cook asparagus." They also dried the vegetable to use in the winter.

With its high tolerance for salt and its preference for sandy soils, wild asparagus is found in sandy or coastal locations in places as varied as England, central Wisconsin, and the steppes of Russia and Poland. It has been grown in Syria, Egypt (where it is pictured on ancient reliefs), and Spain since ancient times. In the sixteenth century, it appeared in France and England, and from there it was brought to America by the early colonists.

Besides enjoying it as a tasty vegetable, the early cultivators believed asparagus had certain medicinal properties. The Greeks and Romans valued asparagus as a diuretic and gentle laxative. The English herbalist Culpepper made much more extravagant claims; he declared that asparagus could be used to "clear the sight, ease the toothache, and help the sciatica."

Asparagus spears are candied in China. In other areas of the world, seeds are used to make a coffee substitute and are fermented to produce an alcoholic drink. But it is as a delicious vegetable that asparagus is so widely popular. Today the Dutch and Italians grow a purple variety; the white *argenteiul* of France is considered tops by gourmets, and the green shades of the Washington strains are found everywhere in the United States.

What Asparagus Likes Best

Asparagus *(Asparagus officinalis)* is an edible member of the lily family. Despite its deserved reputation as a gourmet vegetable and its high market price, it is a hardy plant and is widely cultivated by home gardeners. The main requirement for growing asparagus is a little patience; you have to wait one or two growing seasons after planting before you can begin harvesting.

Choosing a Site

Although asparagus *can* be grown almost anywhere, good production is based on a carefully chosen site. Plant your asparagus where it will be neither crowded (especially by trees) nor in the way. Remember, asparagus is a perennial, so plan for a permanent location. Allow four feet between the asparagus row and any other planting. Some gardeners put all their asparagus in a single row along the edge of the garden or in a row dividing the flower garden from the vegetable garden. The tall summer and fall foliage makes a pleasant background for an area of colorful flowers. Do not put your bed where the plants will shade nearby crops, unless you want to use that shade to advantage when you need a cool spot to put in midsummer lettuce or other plants that require some shade.

Asparagus itself requires full sun; a slight slope facing south will help to give it an early start. It should not be subjected to strong winds. If a windy location is all you have, it may be necessary to stake the plants once the harvesting season is over.

Ideally, the soil should be a well-drained, rich, sandy loam; heavier clay soils should be conditioned with plenty of organic matter. If you have no place to put your asparagus but in a poorly drained spot, raised beds can help a great deal. To make a raised bed, dig the soil deeply. Add additional organic soil to raise the level of the bed one foot. The sides of the bed can be contained by concrete blocks or railroad ties. Or you can let the sides of the bed slope down naturally. The bed will remain in its loose, "fluffed up" condition as long as you do not walk on it.

Finally, since you may need to irrigate occasionally, a handy water supply can be important.

Relative Sizes of Soil Grains		
Light Soils	*Heavy Soils*	
medium sand	very fine sand	fine silt
fine sand	coarse silt	clay

There are three basic types of soil: sandy soil; silty soil, and clayey soil. Mixtures of the three are called loamy soils. Sandy soils have coarse, gritty individual particles that do not adhere when wet. Clayey soils are sticky when wet and have the finest individual soil particles.

How many plants to grow depends, of course, on how much you like asparagus and how much you plan to freeze, can, or dry. Ten plants per person is an "average" crop, but a family that wants plenty for eating fresh, giving to friends, and for winter keeping can use at least twice that amount.

Starting Plants

You can start your asparagus from seeds or from roots. Growing from seeds is cheaper; growing from roots yields quicker results. When you start from seed, you can plant extra and then select the best plants. Then you will not have to worry about root damage from shipping. In addition, the United States Department of Agriculture is now warning gardeners about a prevalent disease, fusarium rot, and claims that the only way to guarantee disease-free plants is to start with treated seeds. You can treat your own seeds (as described on pages 6-7) and you may be able to obtain free seeds from a gardening friend with an established bed.

The major disadvantage of planting seeds is the wait before the harvest — about three years, or one year more than you will have if you start with roots. In general then, starting your plants from seeds gives you more control over the quality and is quite a bit less expensive, but does take more time and effort.

We started our bed from roots and have not noticed any disease problems, but the bed is only three years old. When we expand it, we plan to experiment with plants started from homegrown seed and some transplants from the wild. I have already spotted a wild asparagus patch on the edge of our alfalfa field.

If you decide to start from roots, you can save money by obtaining some or all of your plants from the wild. Wild asparagus occurs very widely in sunny, open locations such as old fields and in sandy soil along riverbanks. Also, it often is found along roadsides. These plants may have been polluted from automotive exhausts or defoliants and should not be eaten; however, the roots can be transplanted to your garden. Wild asparagus is not easy to spot in the early spring but can be recognized easily in the summer or fall by the tall feathery foliage that is distinctive to asparagus. So locate a patch in the year preceding your planting time.

Some authorities suggest that varieties growing in the wild have developed natural immunities to help the plants fight off disease. Wild spears tend to be thinner than garden asparagus, but many find them more highly flavored. Euell Gibbons, the famed connoisseur of wild asparagus, admitted that his preference for the flavor of wild asparagus may stem from his fond childhood memories of gathering the wild plant. Wild asparagus is botanically identical to the domestic kind, but the taste does, in my experience, vary slightly. Perhaps the flavor is more concentrated in the smaller, thinner shoots. Good care and good soil will increase the size of the spears after they are transplanted.

In the early spring, dig the wild roots, taking a clump of earth at least a foot across and as deep as you can go — at least a foot deep — for each plant. Some root damage is inevitable since the roots spread laterally for several feet, and the roots in a clump will be intertwined. Remove any weeds, then plant the soil ball in a trench in the garden with the soil ball and the roots several inches deeper than where you found them. Firm the soil, water, and treat as you would any one-year root.

Asparagus Acutifolius

Did you know that common asparagus has a wild, more exotic cousin? Called *Asparagus acutifolius,* it is found growing wild in dry and sunny locations around the Mediterranean Sea and is distinguished by small thorns along the stalks. Europeans use it as a substitute for ordinary garden asparagus; some prefer it because it is very aromatic. Gourmets prize it as an ingredient in omelets, or seasoned with oil and lemon juice.

If you want to begin your bed by purchasing year-old bare root crowns, select a variety suited to your area and one resistant to asparagus rust. Here are some recommended varieties. Call your local county extension office for more specific recommendations for growing in your climate.

- California U.C. 157   West Coast
- Roberts strain of Mary Washington   East and Midwest
- Rutgers Beacon   East and Midwest
- Waltham Washington   East and Midwest
- Viking   Northern regions

Check the listing in the back of this bulletin for suppliers who sell these varieties.

Before starting plants from seeds, you may want to treat the seeds for a protection against fusarium root rot.

- Soak the seeds for two minutes in a solution of one part laundry bleach and four parts water.
- Rinse the seeds for one minute under cool, running water.
- Plant in soil that has not grown asparagus previously.

The seeds can be started indoors or in a garden seedbed. To start indoors, sow the seed twelve to fourteen weeks before transplanting in the spring when the soil warms up (late December in the Southwest and mid-February in the East).

Use potting soil or a mixture of peat moss, vermiculite, and compost. Plant the seeds three-quarters of an inch deep in two-inch diameter pots (two seeds per pot) or sow the seeds two inches apart in flats. Cover the flats with clear plastic to create a miniature greenhouse and keep the moisture and temperature stable. The temperature should be kept between 75 and 80°F during the day and about 65°F at night. Remove the plastic once the seedlings appear.

Full sunlight is important to the young seedlings. Artificial lights should be used if the plants receive less than twelve to fourteen hours of sunlight a day.

When the soil has warmed up, transplant your seedlings into a temporary garden location. These new plants are not mature enough to be planted deeply in their permanent location. The young seedlings will look like miniature asparagus plants — very ferny. Although asparagus is hardy and reasonably frost-tolerant, it is a good idea to harden off the plants before transplanting. Ten days before you are ready to transplant, cut back on the amount of water and fertilizer you supply. Leave the seedlings outdoors for a few hours each day in a sheltered, sunny location. Gradually build up the time the plants are left outside until they are out night and day. Then you are ready to transplant. Select a temporary location and space the seedlings three inches apart in rows two and one-half feet apart. Only the hardiest of these plants will be selected for the permanent bed.

To start outdoors, sow the seed in a nursery plot of good soil about two weeks before the time tomatoes are normally put in the garden in your area. Select a temporary location and place the seeds one inch deep and three inches apart in the row, with rows two and one-half feet apart. Since asparagus seed is slow to germinate, you may want to mix in some radish seeds to sow in the same row. The radishes will come up early to mark the row and help you see where to weed. Plant three to four seeds for each crown you will want in the permanent bed, and thin to leave the best seedlings.

Whether started indoors or out, the plants will be ready to be moved to their permanent location the following spring. When the plants are still dormant and the ground has thawed, carefully dig the roots with the soil ball intact and plant in prepared trenches.

Look for wild asparagus in the summer or fall in sunny open locations, like the edges of old fields. The tall, feathery green foliage is very distinctive.

Making the Permanent Asparagus Bed

Asparagus spears have been known to grow ten inches in one day, and there are records of shoots weighing a third of a pound each! These plants are supported by powerful roots that often extend five or six feet downward and almost that far to each side. This kind of growth requires a well-prepared site as well as continued attention. Your soil should be rich with organic matter. A soil test to check on the acidity and the levels of nitrogen, phosphorus, and potassium will also help in planning. If you do not have access to a home garden soil test kit, get a soil sample container from your county extension agent, take a sample in the summer before planting, and send it in to be analyzed.

Soil Preparation

In the fall prior to planting roots, till in rich organic material such as manure, compost, or animal bedding, or sow a green manure crop. A green manure, or cover, crop is a technique for growing your own fertilizer by growing a crop simply to till into the ground. This will add organic matter and nutrients to the soil. Winter vetch or rye are good green manures. If you are planning to till in leaves, corncobs, animal bedding, or any other relatively coarse material, shredding prior to working them into the soil is sometimes helpful.

If your soil test has indicated a deficiency, add rock phosphate, bone meal, greensand, or wood ashes for phosphorus; wood ashes or greensand for potassium; or an organic fertilizer, such as cottonseed meal, if nitrogen levels are low. If the test shows an acid soil (any pH lower than 6.5 or 6.8) add lime, preferably dolomite for its magnesium content. In clay soils, five and one-half pounds of dolomite will raise the pH of 100 square feet one degree. Light, sandy soils will require only two pounds per 100 square feet. The lime will also improve the soil texture by binding soil particles and allowing air and moisture to be absorbed more readily.

In early spring in the North, or in late fall in the South, till or cultivate deeply to destroy all the weeds and work in the cover crop. Then you will be ready to plant.

Compost

The use of compost is recommended several places in this bulletin because it is a versatile and very inexpensive fertilizer — it usually costs you nothing. Compost is a mixture of organic materials, like kitchen garbage, leaves, weeds, wood ashes, grass clippings, sawdust, manure, or anything else that will naturally decompose. You can produce compost in a bin made of wood, concrete blocks, a cage of chicken wire or fencing, or in a pile. It can be made at any time of the year though the process is quicker in the warm months. "Recipes" vary; but shredding materials, keeping the pile moist, and turning it once in a while do accelerate the process. The end result will be a balanced, natural fertilizer that will add humus, basic nutrients, and trace minerals to the garden.

Caring for the Roots

If the plants have arrived in the mail, open them at once. Sprinkle the roots with water and cover them with a layer of moss or damp newspaper. Keep the stock in a cool place until you are ready to plant, but plan to plant as soon as possible. Take care not to expose the roots to the drying sun or wind.

Before planting the roots, some gardeners soak them overnight in a mixture of water and well-matured compost and plant only when the sky is overcast or in the evening. Strange as it may seem, the best time for putting in any bare root transplant is on a gloomy, cool day with a heavy mist or light drizzle. If you are planting more than one row, cover and water these roots before going to the next row.

Digging the Trench

Opinions do vary about the best way to set in asparagus roots. To trench or not to trench is the big question.

Some recent gardening books advocate the simple "no-trench" method. To plant by this method, you mark your row, open a shallow furrow, and plant the roots so that the crowns — the points where the roots converge — are about a half inch below the surface of the ground. Then you cover and firm the soil surface. This method is easy but has one major drawback: the roots are so close to the surface that cultivating and weeding become very difficult. Also, incorporating the necessary amounts of organic materials will be impossible with the roots laced so shallowly. You can grow asparagus with the no-trench method, but probably your harvest will not be those two-inch-thick spears that keep coming year after year!

Most experts, therefore, recommend the tried-and-true trench method. The asparagus trench can be twelve to fifteen inches wide and from twelve to eighteen inches deep. Allow four to five feet between trenches.

If you want to extend your harvest over the longest possible period, vary the depth of your trench. In the spring, the plants that are nearest the surface will send up shoots for an early harvest. Those planted a little deeper will produce later, and the deepest roots will come up later still. You can add about three weeks to the harvest in this way.

Here is how to dig a trench for planting the asparagus at different depths. Dig a trench eighteen inches deep and fifteen inches wide for one-third of the bed. As you remove dirt, put the top five inches of the soil on a ridge on one side of the trench, the bottom ten inches on the other side. You will use some of this ridge of soil (the "top" soil) to fill in the trench once the asparagus is in place; the rest of the ridge of soil will be used to fill in the trench during the growing season, as the shoots emerge.

Dig the second third of the bed twelve inches deep and fifteen inches wide. As you remove the dirt, put the top five inches of dirt on one side of the trench, the bottom seven inches on the other side. For the last third of the bed, dig a trench nine inches deep and fifteen inches wide.

Planting the Roots

Fill the bottom eight inches of the deepest part of the trench with compost, well-rotted manure, or rich topsoil. Add seven inches of compost to the second third of the trench, four inches to the shallow end of the trench. Make a slight (one-inch to two-inch) mound every eighteen inches along the trench. Place an asparagus root crown carefully over each mound, spreading the roots out in a circle around the crown, making sure that the small buds on each root are

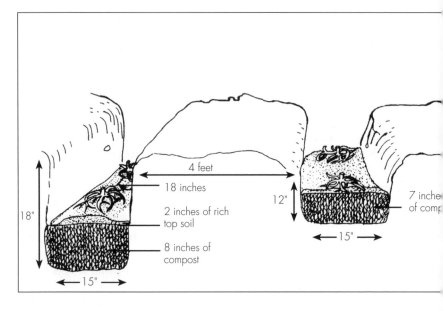

facing up. Two inches of good soil should be placed over the crowns and firmed by hand. Using the "top" soil you dug from the trench, fill in between each mound so that the soil in each third of the trench is level, then water well. Fill in the rest of the trench gradually during the first growing season as the shoots appear. By June, the ridged-up soil should be in the trench, and the entire bed should be level.

During this first season it is especially important not to let the roots dry out. Water once a week, if necessary, enough to wet the soil eight inches deep. Too much water is also harmful — do not let water stand in the trench.

In the spring, the plants that are nearest the surface will send up shoots for an early harvest. Those a little deeper produce later, and the deepest roots come up later still. These later-producing plants, of course, can be harvested a corresponding length of time longer at the end of the season.

You can make the planting simpler by digging the entire trench fifteen inches deep, yet still extend the harvest by using mulch. After you have planted your asparagus as described above, put about five inches of a heavy mulch, such as shredded leaves, over the whole bed. Early in the spring, rake the mulch away from those rows that you want to produce first. The soil will warm up in the bare rows while the mulch will keep the other rows cool and delay the appear-

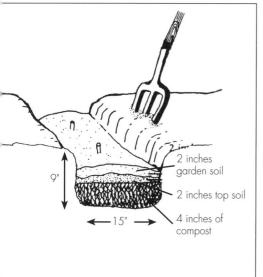

2 inches garden soil

2 inches top soil

4 inches of compost

9"

← 15" →

If you vary the depth of your trench, you can extend your harvest period. Layering the bottom of the trench with compost will give the new root crowns a good start.

ance of shoots. It is important to remove all but a fine layer of mulch as soon as the first spears begin to show. This will keep slugs away from the emerging spears. Also, shoots coming up through heavy mulch sometimes have a tendency to curl over.

Digging your entire trench fifteen inches deep has the additional advantage of keeping the asparagus roots deep enough to enable you to use a rototiller for cultivation.

Cultivation

A productive asparagus plant has a balance between healthy roots and foliage growth. Both are essential for steady, long-term production. Roots need space; do not plant any other deeply rooted crop within four feet of any asparagus row. After the first season, the deep roots of the asparagus plant will normally draw in enough moisture. However, if dry spells occur, two inches of water applied every two weeks should be sufficient.

It is important to keep the beds weed-free; be especially careful to prevent perennial weeds, such as dock and dandelion, from getting established. In the early spring, weed control and plant feeding can be assisted by tilling or shallowly working in manure or other fertilizers or soil conditioners applied the previous fall. The dried

Wood Ashes

If you are one of the many who is reducing your fuel bills by heating with wood, do not throw away the ashes; they will help your asparagus grow. Store them out of the rain or spread over the bed as a mulch. In the spring, stored ashes can be mixed with other fertilizing materials or put as a barrier around the bed to repel crawling insects. Ashes not only contain 1.5% phosphorus and about 7% potassium (which asparagus plants require), they are alkaline and help to maintain the right pH in the bed. So save your ashes and ask your neighbors to save theirs, too.

asparagus ferns from the previous season should be tilled in. A light mulch, especially after the first of June, will discourage weed growth and keep the soil loose. Weeds that do appear should be removed as soon as possible. After the cutting season, a heavy mulch of nonacid materials (straw, grass clippings, ground corncobs, well-rotted sawdust) will help keep weeds down and protect soil moisture during the warm months. In the fall, apply manure or other organic fertilizers.

Never cut or remove the foliage until the asparagus has become completely dormant; these ferns produce the energy that the roots store. Only the female plants produce berries (seeds). If you are not trying to save seed for new plants, remove the seeds as soon as they appear.

Insects and Diseases

Although a healthy asparagus bed may not be bothered by insect damage or disease, you should know how to spot trouble early — and do something about it.

Insects

The most widely reported difficulty is with the common asparagus beetle. This pest injures the spears during the harvest season and attacks the fully grown tops later. The adult, about a quarter of an inch long, is a dull, blue black with three orange yellow squares along each wing. In the larval stage, its soft, wrinkled, wormlike body is about a half of an inch long, colored olive green to dark grey, with black legs and head. The beetle winters in weeds or other

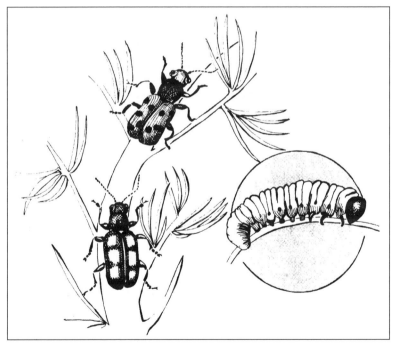

The spotted asparagus beetle (top) has a reddish body with dark spots. The common asparagus beetle (bottom) has a dull, blue black body with six orange yellow spots. Both are about ¼ inch long. The grub of both beetles is a white caterpillar about ½ inch long.

rubbish around the garden, then emerges in the spring to feed on the developing spears and lay small, elongated, black eggs in rows. Later, both adults and larvae attack the fully developed plants. If left unchecked, these pests can cause crooked and unsightly shoots and reduced yields the following season.

When checking for the common asparagus beetle in its caterpillar stage, you do have to look carefully. It is big enough to be seen, but its colors blend well with the plant. Removal of weeds, trash, and other hibernating sites from around the bed should help keep this pest away. It is also a good idea to turn over the soil around the plants in the fall to expose the beetles.

Planting tomatoes near your asparagus bed is often recommended since asparagus beetles find the strong tomato aroma objectionable. Asparagus will also help keep tomato nematodes in check, which makes this combination a good example of "companion planting."

The beetles can be handpicked early in the morning when it is too cool for them to fly. We find that bordering our patch with tomatoes together with a program of early-in-the-season hand-picking is sufficient pest control for our asparagus. A rotenone dust can be applied as needed. This organic pest control has no long-term harsh residues and is effective against the larval and adult stages of most beetles. Pyrethrum and ryania are the names of two other botanical, or natural, insecticides that can be used if other measures are not effective.

East of the Mississippi, the spotted asparagus beetle may be a problem. This bug is distinguished by its reddish brown or orange color and its six black spots on each wing. It is as large as the common asparagus beetle — about ¼ inch long. Control is the same as for the common asparagus beetle.

Japanese beetles may attack the foliage in sufficient numbers to be a concern. If so, they are probably doing damage elsewhere in the garden and can best be countered with the biological control called milky spore disease, which can be purchased at most garden supply stores. Or you can set up some Japanese beetle traps, also available commercially. Sometimes dusting the asparagus foliage with lime is enough to deter them.

Japanese beetles are now present from southern Maine to South Carolina and Georgia and westward to Michigan and Missouri. Oddly enough, new housing developments are especially susceptible to infestation because imported turf may harbor these beetles.

The colorful Japanese beetle (top right) has a metallic green body with copper-colored wing covers and grows to about ¼ inch in size. The grubs (left) are white with brown heads; they grow to about an inch in size and are often transported in turf. Slugs (bottom right) are another enemy of asparagus. The adult slug has dark spots on an inch-long, yellowish body. The month-old slug is brown with dark spots.

The "new soil" in these tracts often is lacking in the natural enemies of Japanese beetles.

In moist weather slugs may present a problem, especially if your bed is mulched. The slugs can be turned aside by spreading a barrier of wood ashes around the bed; this acts as an irritant to their soft bodies (and the same wood ash barrier will also discourage cutworms). Handpicking can be aided by laying a board near the asparagus at night, then removing the slugs from under it in the morning. Ashes and handpicking have worked best for us; but you can try trapping slugs, too. Just fill saucers or jar lids with beer mixed with a little flour and set them out. The slugs like the beer but find it difficult to leave the sticky solution. Clean and refill the traps once in a while.

Diseases

Asparagus is susceptible to two serious diseases: asparagus rust and fusarium root rot. Asparagus rust is a fungus disease that caused much destruction in the late nineteenth and early twentieth centuries, until disease-resistant varieties were introduced. The

Martha and Mary Washington asparagus varieties, originally developed to be rust-resistant, increasingly are attacked by new rust strains, so one of the newer varieties should be planted. But these plants are resistant only, not immune, so you should know how to spot the disease.

Rust looks like rust — elongated, dusty, orange red or brown spots. They disfigure the shoots and a heavy infestation can cause the tops of the plant to turn yellow and die early. Since the rust spores require dampness, the problem is worse in moist seasons and locations. If rust does occur, be sure to cut all the spears that emerge during the cutting season, even the very small ones that you would normally ignore. In this way, the spores will not have a chance to develop. Then, in the fall, cut affected tops close to the ground and burn them.

According to the USDA, the most serious asparagus disease is another fungal problem — fusarium root rot, which is present at low levels in most soils. This usually causes no difficulties, but if infected seeds or crowns are planted, a rapid buildup of the fungus can be expected. Then the fungus kills feeder roots, plant vigor declines, spear size decreases, and weaker plants may die.

If your beds are declining for no apparent reason, a check for fusarium is in order. Examination must be made below the soil line. Using a trowel, carefully loosen the soil around the roots and look down to the roots. Fusarium is present if the feeder roots (small side roots) are reddish brown, if there are reddish brown spots or streaks on the storage roots (large main roots), or if there are large lesions (sores) on the base of the spears or stalks below the soil level. As with most plant diseases, the symptoms are much more severe when the plants are under stress due to excessively long harvests, poor drainage, weed competition, or insect damage.

If fusarium is the cause of the decline in production of your bed, then you may want to consider digging up your asparagus patch and starting a new one in a different location. There is no cure for fusarium. The USDA asserts that it is difficult to obtain commercial roots free of fusarium root rot fungus and that the best way to avoid it is to plant surface-sterilized seed in disease-free soil. Some seed companies are now trying to make available asparagus seed selected for its resistance to fusarium. However, such seed is not widely available yet, so you may want to sterilize the seeds yourself.

Harvesting

Although commercial growers usually harvest spears when they are eight to twelve inches high, most gardeners feel that asparagus tastes best when the shoots are about five inches tall. If you are more concerned about quantity, you can wait until the spears are mature, eight or nine inches tall. Experiment with harvest sizes; but do harvest before the heads start to open. This will keep the beds in strong production. It may mean daily harvesting in hot weather. Snap or cut the asparagus at ground level, and be careful not to injure the buds below the surface.

How much should you harvest? It depends on the inherent capacity of the plants themselves. There is no real limit to the number of spears that can be harvested. Plants have been known to produce more than a hundred spears per season and a single asparagus spear may grow as much as ten inches in one day under ideal conditions! This explains the need to be attentive to the plants' requirements for space, moisture, and nutrients.

The first year after planting or transplanting roots, harvest only a few spears or none at all. Those first spears may be hard to resist; so if you do harvest, one or two stalks from each plant should be the limit. The second year you can harvest for two weeks, the third year for four weeks, and in the fourth and following years for eight weeks. These are, of course, only general guidelines. The vigor of the plants, as indicated by the number and size of the shoots, should determine the harvest. Small, slender stalks (the size of a pencil orless) should be left alone. Best production may be expected when the bed is from five to ten years old, and the average length of production for a bed is from fifteen to eighteen years. At that point you will have to decide whether declining production warrants putting in a new bed.

To Cut or Not to Cut

Most directions for harvesting asparagus suggest cutting the spears below the soil surface, using a sharp knife. You can even buy a special asparagus knife for this purpose. But cutting involves the risk of damaging nearby roots or buds. And the subsurface ends of the shoots are tough and must be trimmed off. It is much easier just to go down the row and snap the mature spears off at soil level. The asparagus harvested this way will all be tender and easy to clean.

Hot weather may interfere with your harvest when the cutting season is half over, especially if you have used the no-trench method or have staggered planting depths to extend the season. The high temperatures (a week in June with temperatures in the eighties, for example) coupled with the continued harvesting, will cause the plant to overproduce, leading to an eventual decline in plant vigor. You can circumvent this by keeping the soil temperature cool. Ridge five to six inches of soil carefully over the row. This will lower the temperature around the crown and increase spear size. Level the bed with a rake after the last harvest.

Older books on asparagus growing frequently suggest techniques for bleaching or producing a spear with a white base by excluding sunlight from that portion while it is growing. However, modern sources agree that this is extra work for a result that is purely cosmetic. Naturally green asparagus is more tender, better flavored, and richer in vitamins. Blanched spears must be peeled and this further reduces the vitamin content.

What If the Bed Is Not Producing Well?

Poor asparagus production is usually the result of a few common problems.

- Insufficient or unbalanced soil nutrition
- Insect or disease problems
- Lack of moisture or bad drainage
- Declining vigor due to plant aging

Soil Nutrition

Test the soil regularly (every two years) to make sure that enough nutrients are present and that the soil is not too acid. Remember to keep the pH in the 6.5 to 6.8 range. Asparagus requires a high level of potassium, so make sure your fertilizing program contains enough of that ingredient.

Avoid overapplication of fertilizers high in nitrogen. Too much nitrogen will stimulate top growth at the expense of root development. Balanced growth is best insured by using an organic fertilizer or compost which releases nutrients slowly and increases the humus content of the soil.

Field Test for Soil pH

Using rainwater to moisten the soil sample, shape it into a ball. Split the sample and slip a piece of litmus paper between the halves. Blue shades indicate alkaline soils, reds indicate acid soils.

Soil testing kit

Insect or Disease Problems

Damage from insect infestations and plant disease can be minimized if the plants are carefully inspected before planting and inspected regularly to spot trouble early. If you start from seed, select only the most vigorous seedlings to transplant. Grow plenty and be ruthless in discarding the weaklings. If you buy crowns, deal only with reputable suppliers, avoid bargains, and choose the disease-resistant variety recommended for your area.

If the bugs do start chewing, take countermeasures before populations have a chance to build up. One early morning of hand-picking bugs can be more effective than a lot of spraying or dusting once the pests have gone through a population explosion. Don't forget, there are many natural predators for asparagus pests, such as ladybug larvae and chalcid wasps, that will be working for you in your garden. Old-time gardeners even used chickens to clean up the offending asparagus beetles; but if you try this method, remember that chickens may also feast on friendly insects, as well as your early lettuce and strawberries!

Lack of Moisture or Bad Drainage

Asparagus roots need water but not too much water. If your soil is especially heavy (high clay content), or if the bed is located in a depression, drainage may be bad, and the roots will have difficulty obtaining enough air. Humus (decayed organic matter) in the soil will help keep the soil loose, promote air circulation and water drainage, and at the same time keep the soil from becoming too dry. A mulch on the surface will help towards the same ends.

Remember that asparagus may need water in dry weather even after the harvest season is over. Of course, supplying sufficient water is especially important in the first season when the plants are just getting established.

Plant Aging

Claims are made about asparagus plants lasting for a lifetime. Records of good production for thirty years or more certainly can be found, but most beds will need to be replaced after sixteen or seventeen years, and some will do well only for a decade. Asparagus beds that are seriously weakened by disease may have to be replaced completely. Production tells the tale. If you are still harvesting plenty of good asparagus after twenty-five years, take pride in your efforts and leave the bed alone.

Cooking Asparagus

Many claim that the best way to get full flavor and nutrition from fresh vegetables is to eat them raw. You can eat asparagus right out of the garden — just snap off the tender tips and savor that fresh asparagus flavor. Or include the raw tips in salads, fresh or marinated.

Raw or cooked, asparagus should be used right after harvesting. The quick growth of the plant is associated with chemical changes that continue after the spears are snapped off. The soluble proteins and sugar are altered to produce simpler compounds that have a bitter taste. By refrigerating the spears at once, the chemical changes are halted and the delicate sweetness of fresh asparagus is preserved. Tie the spears in a bundle and stand the bottoms in about an inch of water. They will retain good flavor for a day or so if kept cool.

Of course, I have a lot of fun growing asparagus and appreciate the delicate beauty of the patch at different times of the year. But there is nothing like the enjoyment of a well-prepared meal featuring this vegetable treat. At our farm in central Pennsylvania, we begin harvesting asparagus in May, and for two months we eat asparagus as often as we want — and that means several times a week. Do we get tired of it? No, mainly because asparagus is such a versatile vegetable and lends itself to a variety of tasty dishes. Here are just a few of the ways in which asparagus is enjoyed at the Peaceful Peach Farm.

Keep asparagus fresh in the refrigerator by storing in a jar with the asparagus bottoms standing in about an inch of water.

BASIC COOKED ASPARAGUS

Tie the asparagus spears together with string so that the bottoms are level. Place the bundle upright in a deep pot with the asparagus bottoms in about one and one-half inches of boiling water. Cover tightly and cook for about twelve minutes or until the spears are tender. Drain and serve.

As a variation on this, you can save the cooking water and combine it with a half teaspoon of salt and one cup of bread crumbs sautéed in butter. Pour this over the asparagus tips.

The freshly cooked asparagus can be seasoned with butter and Parmesan cheese or oil with lemon juice or tamari (a concentrated soy sauce available in most health food stores). Of course, freshly cooked asparagus is delicious when served with a simple hollandaise sauce.

BLENDER-MADE HOLLANDAISE SAUCE

3   egg yolks
¼   teaspoon salt
2   tablespoons lemon juice
dash cayenne
½   cup melted butter

Mix all the ingredients in a blender, except the butter, which is added gradually in a steady stream while the blender is operating.

SERVES FOUR WITH ONE POUND OF COOKED ASPARAGUS.

HERBED LEMON BUTTER

This is another favorite accompaniment for asparagus.

¼   cup butter
1½ tablespoons lemon juice
1½ tablespoons sesame seeds
1   tablespoon fresh parsley, minced
1   tablespoon fresh basil *or* marjoram

Melt the butter and stir in the other ingredients.

SERVES FOUR WITH ONE POUND OF COOKED ASPARAGUS.

CREAM OF ASPARAGUS SOUP

1   pound fresh asparagus
4   cups chicken *or* vegetable stock
salt and pepper to taste
2   tablespoons butter
2   tablespoons flour
1   cup half-and-half *or* whole milk

Trim the butt ends from the asparagus, remove the tips, and cut the stalks into short, one-inch pieces. Place the asparagus in a pan with the stock, add salt and pepper. Bring to a boil, cover, and simmer on a low heat. Remove the tips after five minutes and continue to simmer the stalks for another eight minutes. Set the tips aside and process the stalks in a blender or press through a sieve.

Melt the butter, stir in the flour, and cook together for two to three minutes. Stir in the blended asparagus, add the half-and-half, and cook gently for two to three minutes. Serve garnished with the asparagus tips.

SERVES FOUR TO SIX.

BAKED ASPARAGUS

2   tablespoons butter
2   tablespoons flour
1½   cups milk
2   cups grated cheese
2   pounds cooked asparagus
1   cup bread crumbs *or* sunflower seeds

In a heavy skillet, melt the butter over low heat. Blend in the flour. Slowly add the milk and cook for about five minutes, stirring until smooth. Add half the cheese to the sauce.

In a greased casserole dish, arrange alternate layers of sauce and asparagus. Top with the rest of the cheese and the bread crumbs or sunflower seeds. Brown lightly in the oven (about twenty minutes at 350°F).

SERVES SIX.

ASPARAGUS CREPES

The secret of making good crepes is using a well-seasoned pan. The best crepe pan of all is one that is used only for making crepes. It is never washed; after each use it is merely wiped out. This recipe calls for a seven-inch pan.

Crepes:

3	eggs
1½	cups milk
½	teaspoon salt
1	cup flour
1	tablespoon melted butter
	butter to grease the pan

Filling:

2	pounds cooked asparagus
½	pound grated cheese

Make the crepe batter by beating the eggs with the milk and salt. Gradually add the flour, beating until smooth. (You can mix this up in a blender, if you prefer.) Stir in the melted butter.

Melt a small piece of butter in a crepe pan or small skillet. Pour three tablespoons of batter into the pan and tilt the pan to distribute the batter evenly. Cook over medium heat for one minute, until the crepe turns a golden color. Turn it over to brown the other side.

Cut the asparagus stalks in half. Place a small amount of cheese in the center of each crepe. Add four pieces of asparagus. Fold the crepe around the filling to make a rectangle. Briefly sauté the filled crepes in butter. Serve immediately. This is good with spicy tomato, mushroom, or cream sauce.

MAKES FIFTEEN CREPES.

GRILLED ASPARAGUS SANDWICH

Place cooked asparagus spears on slices of whole wheat bread covered with mayonnaise. Add a dash of lemon juice, paprika, fresh dill or basil, and tomato slices. Grill.

ASPARAGUS SOUFFLÉ

3   tablespoons oil
3   tablespoons flour
2   tablespoons chopped fresh parsley *or* ½ teaspoon dried basil
1   cup milk
4   eggs, separated
2½ cups cooked asparagus, cut in 1-inch pieces

Blend the oil, flour, and herbs in the top of a double boiler. Gradually add the milk, and mix thoroughly. Cook, stirring, until the mixture thickens slightly. Cool to lukewarm. Gradually beat in the egg yolks. Add the asparagus, then fold in the stiffly beaten egg whites. Turn into an oiled soufflé dish. Bake at 325°F for forty-five minutes or until set.

SERVES FOUR.

SKILLET ASPARAGUS

2   pounds cooked asparagus
3   tablespoons olive oil
salt
pepper
lemon juice

Slice the asparagus on the diagonal into ¼-inch slices. Heat the oil in a large, heavy skillet. Add asparagus, and stir fry over high heat for about two minutes. Add salt, pepper, and lemon juice to taste. Serve immediately.

SERVES SIX.

Cats Love It!

Explanations for this phenomenon are scarce and people who have not observed it are skeptical, but cats delight in asparagus, raw or cooked. Usually, dogs will not touch it — unless it is dripping with butter, in which case you know what they are after. But there is something about this vegetable that cats seem to hunger for. Now you can get cat food right out of your garden!

ASPARAGUS TEMPURA

Horseradish Sauce:

4	tablespoons prepared horseradish
1½	tablespoons lemon juice
½	teaspoon salt
½	teaspoon pepper
½	teaspoon paprika
½	cup plain yogurt

Batter:

3	eggs
2	tablespoons soy sauce
1¼	cups water
1⅔	cups flour
2	tablespoons sugar
2	pounds cooked asparagus
	oil for deep frying

Prepare the horseradish sauce by combining the horseradish with the lemon juice and seasonings. Fold in the yogurt. Set aside.

To make the batter, first beat the eggs. Then add the soy sauce and water. Gradually add the flour, sugar, and salt. Beat until smooth.

Drain the cooked asparagus. Blot with paper towels until completely dry.

Heat the oil in a heavy skillet. Using a pair of tongs, dip the asparagus into the batter to coat lightly and add to the hot oil. Deep fry a few pieces of asparagus at a time. Fry for about three minutes, or until golden brown. Drain. Serve with horseradish dipping sauce.

SERVES EIGHT AS AN APPETIZER OR SIX AS A MAIN DISH SERVED WITH RICE.

MARINATED COOKED ASPARAGUS

2   tablespoons olive oil
2   tablespoons vinegar
1   teaspoon honey
¼   teaspoon salt
1   crumbled bay leaf
12   cooked asparagus spears

Mix together the oil, vinegar, honey, and seasonings. Place the asparagus spears in a shallow dish, pour the marinade over them, and refrigerate for several hours, turning the asparagus once.

SERVES FOUR.

Sauce That Asparagus

There are those who think it sacrilege to eat asparagus any other way but in stalk form, napped with hollandaise or a lemon-butter sauce. However, if you have a surplus of asparagus, it is nice to view it in some other fashion after it appears night after night during the height of the season. Asparagus puree makes a lovely soup with a chicken stock base and the addition of potato, curry powder, and shrimp. Mixed with cream cheese, it is a flavorful stuffing for mushrooms or strudel dough. The sauce can be added to hollandaise to serve with hot salmon or to mayonnaise to mask a cold salmon. We like asparagus as a bed for baked oysters, and our asparagus crepes can be frozen for future use.

Spread asparagus puree over the bottom of a pie shell and fill it with an onion-cheese-custard mixture — or incorporate it into a ham mousse. The mixture I use for the former is a quarter cup of sautéed onions, half a cup of grated cheese, three eggs beaten with two cups of milk, seasoned with salt, pepper, and a half teaspoon of prepared mustard.

Method: Break off and discard the tough bottom part of the stems and cut the stalks into one-inch lengths. Cook in boiling salted water for three to four minutes. Drain and put through food mill or puree in blender or food processor. Asparagus puree can be frozen.

Three cups of asparagus cut in half-inch lengths equal one cup puree.

Marjorie Blanchard, *Sauce It!*, Garden Way Publishing

Preserving Asparagus

While many people feel that asparagus can be appreciated truly only when fresh, others cannot be without it in the off-season. If you want to preserve your asparagus, you can freeze, can, or dry this versatile vegetable.

To freeze asparagus, first blanch the spears, a few at a time, in water that is kept boiling. Blanch for three minutes, then soak in ice water for ten minutes. While the vegetables are blanching, have a cookie sheet chilling in the freezer. Drain, then lay the spears in a single layer on the chilled cookie sheet, not touching each other. Quickly place the asparagus in the coldest part of the freezer. Remove when completely frozen and place in tightly closed plastic bags.

To can, wash and remove the tough ends. Place the spears upright in a pot filled with water — enough to reach to just below the tips. Boil for three minutes. Or cut the asparagus into pieces (about one inch long) and boil for two to three minutes. Pack into clean jars and fill the jars with boiling water. Process for forty minutes at ten pounds of pressure.

For best drying results, dry right after picking. Wash, drain dry, and split lengthwise in half or cut into half-inch slices. Blanch in boiling water for three minutes or steam for five minutes. Blot dry with paper towels. Dry in strong sunlight or in a dehydrator. To use, add to soups, marinate, or reconstitute by simmering for thirty minutes.

Suppliers

If possible, it is best to buy seeds or plants that have been produced in your area; they are more suited to local climate and conditions. If you cannot find asparagus locally, check out these suppliers.

Roots

Buy only year-old roots; two-year and three-year crowns are only more expensive, not better.

Daisy Farms
269-782-6321
www.daisyfarms.net

Nourse Farms
413-665-2658
www.noursefarms.com

Seed

The number of seeds you buy will be much greater than the number of plants you want. This will allow you to be selective with young seedlings.

Main Street Seed and Supply
866-229-3276
www.mainstreetseedandsupply.com

Victory Seed Company
503-829-3126
www.victoryseeds.com